On the theory of
KARMA
Death & Reincarnation

R S Sethi

Vitasta

Vitasta Publishing Pvt. Ltd.
New Delhi

Published by
Renu Kaul Verma for Vitasta Publishing Pvt. Ltd.
2/15, Ansari Road, Daryaganj, New Delhi - 110 002

ISBN 10 81-89766-38-4
ISBN 13 978-81-89766-38-2

Reprint 2011

Typeset and Cover Design by Vitasta Publishing Pvt. Ltd.
Printed by Vits Press, New Delhi

Contents

1

THEORY OF KARMA

The law of cause and effect forms an integral part of Hindu philosophy. This law is termed as 'Karma', which means to 'act'. The Pali term 'Karma' literally means action or doing. In Sanskrit, 'Karma' means 'volitional action that is undertaken deliberately or knowingly.

The theory of Karma harps on the Newtonian principle that every action produces an equal and opposite reaction. Karma could be both the activities of the body or the mind, irrespective of the consideration whether the performance brings fruition immediately or at a later stage. However, the involuntary or the reflex actions cannot be called Karma.

Hindu philosophy, which believes in life after death, holds the doctrine that if the Karma of an individual is good enough, the next birth will be rewarding, and if not, the person may actually devolve and degenerate into a lower life form.

In order to achieve good Karma, it is important to live life according to *Dharma* or what is right. The trail of Karma is indeed intricate, jagged and inscrutable. Sudama, a friend of Lord Krishna, beautifully summed it up as under:

> 'The working of Karma seems so complex
> We too, the students of the same Guru
> He (Krishna) became the king of this earth
> While I have nothing even to eat
> He used to play with monkeys in Gokul
> And I used to fetch wood for the teacher's house
> 'Now he sits on the throne today
> While I possess only a begging bowl and a stick in hand.'

The Law of Karma is the law of action and reaction, cause and effect and effort and destiny. It is essentially as under:

Jo Jas Karai So Tas Fal Chakha
(As you sow, so shall you reap)

Features

- This law is Eternal and is co-terminus with the existence of the Universe.
- This law is Universal and is applicable to all people irrespective of caste and creed.
- This law is applicable in all the generations and eras of the earthly cycles namely *Satyug*, *Treta*, *Dwapar* and *Kaliyug* and in all the centuries—past, present and future.
- This law is cent per cent perfect. There are no condionalities or amendments.

- There is not a single exception to this law. It is equally applicable to either the omnipotent God (*Nirankar*) or its incarnation in the human form (*Sakar*).

The application of the law is beyond manipulation, intervention or corruptibility.

CLASSIFICATION

Karma can be broadly classified into the following:

Kriyaman Karma

Kriyaman Karma relates to action(s) done on the spur of the moment or time which almost instantaneously bears fruit and results in reaction. As, for instance, you drink water and your thirst is quenched for the time being. If you are hungry, you eat and almost immediately your hunger is satisfied. Your sexual desire is satiated once you have sex with a woman.

Sanchit Karma (Cumulative Karma)

Sanchit Karma relates to actions done but not yet ripe to give fruits immediately or on the spot but would take some time. They remain in balance and often get accumulated over a period of time. Until their eventual fruition, these Karmas would not be neutralized under any circumstances.

As, for instance, if you appear in an examination today, the results will come out only after some time.

If you troubled your parents in your young age causing considerable anguish to them, your own children may well return the compliment by torturing you likewise in your old age.

Certain actions and effects in the *Kriyaman* Karmas have their maturity date. Till then, they are stored away, kept in abeyance and get accumulated in the balance as *Sanchit* Karmas. But what is certain is that they do their job, without exception, in due course. There is no escaping from it.

Nobody can escape or avoid the punishment for his sinful actions even after many rebirths.

The sinful deeds will remain latent and dormant as *Sanchit* Karmas waiting for the opportune time to confront the person concerned. His sins will ultimately catch up with him even after hundreds of births. Thus, there is neither delay nor any chaos in the realm of God.

Prarabdha Karma (Destiny, Fate, Luck, etc.)

A large number of *Sanchit* Karmas pile up or get credited with a person during his past many births. All of them do not become ripe to give fruits during one life time, and only some of them do so. In other words, some of them get redeemed whilst others get accumulated.

The Karmas which are readily destined to give fruit either on account of luck, fate, fortune or destiny are referred to as *Prarabdha* Karmas.

Although it may take time, the fact remains that no action is lost without reaction, no cause is lost without effect, no effort is lost without destiny and no sin is lost without punishment according to the Law of Karma.

Someday, the *Sanchit* Karmas would ripen into *Prarabdha* from where there is no escape, whatsoever.

Not a single holy or pious deed (*Punya* Karma) would go without reward and not a sinful deed/action (*Paap* Karma) can escape without punishment.

Some people who may have earned and accumulated many pious deeds in their previous births as *Sanchit* Karmas, which have now matured and ripened as *Prarabdha* for this birth, are now enjoying and exhausting them in their present birth. Let them exhaust them now but, thereafter, their present sinful deeds which are slowly accumulating as *Sanchit* Karmas will ultimately ripen and mature in due course. They will start having their dreadful effects soon after all their previous pious deeds have been duly rewarded. So, there may be delay in the House of God, but there would surely be justice at the end of it all.

Types of Persons

Three types of persons exist in the world. These can be broadly categorized as under:

Satvik These are persons of pious mentality and motives.
Rajsik Such persons are of selfish mentality and motives.
Tamsik They are of crooked mentality and motive.

Prarabdha is unavoidable and irrevocable in the case of all these three types of persons. But what is different is the method of facing, accepting, suffering or enjoying the *Prarabdha* with different kinds of people.

A *Satvik* will perform action(s) with a pious and noble mind whether he gets its fruit or not. A *Rajsik* will perform action(s) only after making it sure that he would obtain its fruits which he will not give up at any cost. A *Tamsik* will refuse to perform any action(s) unless he first gets its fruit.

Be that as it may, the fact remains that you will get only that much which is destined in your *Prarabdha* and nothing more or less than that.

It is a common belief amongst many people that on the sixth day of the birth of a child, the Goddess of Destiny named *Vidhata* comes at night to chart the life course of the new-born and write the destiny as to what is going to happen during the entire life time of that child. This is written on the white, yellow and red papers which are kept arranged for the Goddess.

Nobody can see the Goddess nor can they read what has been written by her. Even Goddess *Vidhata* cannot favor anybody by adding, subtracting or manipulating any item(s) from the Prarabdha that is prescribed strictly according to previous *Kriyaman* Karmas done by him in his previous birth(s) which have now matured and ripened as *Prarabdhas* to be enjoyed or suffered during his present birth. You are eligible or entitled to get only that much which is specifically destined in your *Prarabdha*.

Your *Prarabdha* in your present birth is the direct effect and specifically based and shaped on the *Kriyaman* Karmas of your past birth(s).

Even if you aspire and strenuously strive, it is well nigh impossible to get anything more than what is destined in your *Prarabdha*, under any circumstances.

So this naturally begs a question. If this is the gospel truth, then why should we make any new efforts at all (*Purushartha*) and labor unnecessarily? This can perhaps be best explained by citing a few examples.

Securing a job is a matter of destiny, but having secured one, to sustain it is purely a matter of personal effort(s). Likewise, to obtain a beautiful house is shaped by destiny, but to maintain it properly is again a matter of personal effort. Thus there is no contradiction.

Yesterday's *Purushartha* (efforts—*Kriyaman* Karma) are today's *Prarabdha* (destiny). Today's *Purushartha* is tomorrow's *Prarabdha* and the ccle goes on eternally. In other words, *Purushartha* is the architect of one's own *Prarabdha*. A person has many desires, needs, likes etc. All such human wants have been classified into four categories in our scriptures.

Dharma

This pertains t0o ethics and religion and entails performing *Yagna*, giving alms, donations, undertaking penance, going on pilgrimages, etc.

Artha

This relates to acquisition of wealth and worldly materialistic objects in order to facilitate a better and easy life style.

Kama

Pertains to enjoyment through marriage, having children and maintaining good health.

Moksha

Liberation from the cycle of birth and death.

For Dharma and *Moksha*, a man should always constantly do *Purushartha* (efforts) and should never leave it to *Prarabdha*.

For *Artha* and *Kama*, one should leave them to *Prarabdha* as he is going to get only that much of wealth (*Artha*) and enjoyment (Kama) which is destined in his *Prarabdha* and nothing more in spite of all his *Purushartha*.

There is no subtraction of sinful deeds from pious deeds. If we perform hundred pious deeds and say thirty sinful deeds in a life time, then those thirty sinful deeds will not be subtracted from the hundred pious deeds. The two accounts are maintained separately and cannot be mixed up.

So long as a single *Kriyaman*, *Sanchit* or *Prarabdha* Karma is pending or lying in balance in your account, you are bound to take births. Unfortunately, instead of reducing our *Sanchit* and *Prarabdha* Karmas during our life time in one birth, we, on the contrary keep on creating/adding many more new *Kriyaman* Karmas which get subsequently matured in course of time and come before us as *Prarabdha* Karmas in subsequent birth(s). This is a vicious circle and does not allow us to be free and help in securing *Moksha*, which is the ultimate goal of human life, thereby ridding us of the constant cycle of births and deaths.

So how do we hope to get *Moksha*?

You cannot get *Moksha* so long as there is a single *Kriyaman*, *Sanchit* or *Prarabdha* Karma lying in balance in your account. To obtain *Moksha*, we have to adeptly, during our life time, to wipe out completely all the Karmas somehow before you leave your present human body. Then and then only, you will not be required or compelled to suffer the cycle of birth and death. In this manner, you can secure union (yoga) with God which is the ultimate goal of life. Such a tactful and skilful handling of Karmas with prudence and discrimination is precisely called Yoga.

How to wipe out all these Karmas in one's life time?

You should perform only those *Kriyaman* Karmas which would not be accumulated as *Sanchit* Karmas during your present life time. Thus, you should stop the flow and should not allow any new Karma to be accumulated thereby increasing the present stock of *Sanchit* Karmas which you have earned during your past births.

Thereafter, all the *Sanchit* Karmas in balance, earned and accumulated until now because of your past deeds, should be got completely burnt in the fire of knowledge (*Jnanagni*—self- realization). All *Prarabdha* Karmas have to be totally exhausted by enjoying and/or suffering them during this life time in the present birth. Nothing should be carried forward.

How to stop them?

If we stop performing *Kriyaman* Karmas even for a moment, the results can be devastating, to say the least. Thus, on one side you cannot stop doing *Kriyaman* Karmas, while on the other hand if you do any *Kriyaman* Karma, either good or bad, pious or sinful, you cannot hope to escape the cycle of birth and death by securing *Moksha*.

Then what to do? How can one avoid this seemingly complicated and apparently paradoxical situation and to be free from the bondage of all the Karmas?

The answer lies in performing only such *Kriyaman* Karmas as can be completely enjoyed/suffered and totally exhausted during one's present life time without any carry over for accumulation as *Sanchit* Karmas for subsequent birth(s). The real key is to perform only those *Kriyaman* Karmas, with proper dexterity and discretion, which would have the effect of not adding to the burden of *Sanchit* Karmas to be reckoned for in subsequent birth(s). There are many *Kriyaman* Karmas that are not counted for accumulation as *Sanchit* Karmas. They are seven in number and are listed as under:

- Actions performed innocently in childhood/minor age.
- Actions performed in unconscious, insane and intoxicated state of mind.

- Actions performed in other than human life.
- Actions performed without any bias in mind due to attachment or detachment, like or dislike etc.
- Actions performed without any ego of the doer.
- Actions performed for the good and benefit of the society at large with a benevolent motive.
- Actions performed selflessly with devotion unto God (*Nishkam* Karma). Tulsidas had once observed:

  'Whatever is predestined for you, either your *Prarabdha* will drag you to the right place at the right moment to make it a reality for you, or it will come running on its feet to wherever you are hiding. In any event, until your pre-destined fate has become a reality for you, you cannot escape from the clutches of *Prarabdha*.'

One has to face your *Prarabdha*. You cannot escape from it nor can it be transferred to any one else. Whatever sins he has committed willingly while laughing, he has to suffer them weeping. This is the Law of Karma.

How can Astrology be linked to Karma?

While you cannot change your *Prarabdha* which is the predetermined path in the journey of life, Astrological predictions can give you proper caution and guidance as to how to carry on your life journey smoothly with least possible trouble while performing your *Prarabdha* with your utmost *Purushartha* in the right direction as shown by Astrology.

Merely having information on a variety of subjects does not entitle you to be called *Jnani* in the real sense of the term unless you know your own original eternal real self—a realization of one's own self as to who am I?

The present worldly life span between your physical birth and death is also nothing but a relatively long dream in which your pangs, pains and pleasures are totally false and unreal (*Mithya*). There is no birth or death of your original eternal soul. Your old body goes to the grave and not your eternal immortal self; you yourself continue eternally and changelessly in all your ever changing different mortal bodies.

Truly, it is said:

'Life is real, life is earnest
And the grave is not its goal;
"Dust thou art to Dust returneth"
Was not spoken of the soul
I slept and dreamt that life is beauty
I awoke and found that life is duty.'

In the ultimate sense, Karma means all moral and immoral volition. Involuntary, unintentional or unconscious actions, though technically deeds, do not constitute Karma, because volition, the most important factor in determining Karma, is absent. Karma does not necessarily mean past actions. It embraces both past and present deeds. Hence in one sense, we are the result of what we were; we will be the result of what we are.

This vast Universe is a wheel. Upon it are all creatures that are subject to birth, death and rebirth. Round and round, it turns, and never stops. It is the Wheel of the Brahman. As long as the individual self thinks it is separate from Brahman, it revolves upon the wheel in bondage to the cycle of birth, death and rebirth. But when through the grace of Brahma it realizes its identity with him, it revolves upon the wheel no longer. It achieves immortality.

(*Svetasvatara Upanishad* [*Prabhavananda*],118)

2

DEATH

Death is the end of the life of a biological organism. It may refer to the end of life as either an event or condition. Many factors can cause or contribute to an organism's death. These include disease, malnutrition, accidents and ageing.

Death was once defined as the cessation of heart beat (cardiac arrest) and breathing.

But recent advances have rendered this definition somewhat inadequate because breathing and heart beat can sometimes be restarted. This is now called 'clinical death'.

Without a functioning heart or lungs, life can sometimes be sustained with a combination of life support systems, organ transplants and use of artificial pacemaker.

Today, where a definition of death is required, doctors and coroners usually turn to 'brain death' or 'biological death'. People are considered dead when the electrical activity in their brain ceases (persistent vegetative state). It is presumed that the stoppage of electrical activity indicates the end of consciousness.

However, suspension of consciousness must be permanent, and not transient, as occurs during sleep, and especially a coma. In the case of sleep, EEG's can easily tell the difference. Courts have ruled that 'It appears that once brain death has been determined.... no criminal or civil liability will result from disconnecting the life-support devices.'

Even by 'whole-brain' criteria, the determination of brain death can be complicated. EEG's can detect spurious electrical impulses, while certain drugs, hypoglycemia, hypoxia or hypothermia can suppress or even stop brain activity on a temporary basis. Because of this, hospitals have protocols for determining brain death involving EEG's at widely separated intervals under defined conditions.

A person is not to be assumed dead unless there are clear and obvious indications that death has occurred. These indications include decapitation, rigor mortis, livor mortis (blood pooling in the part of the body at least elevation), decomposition and other bodily damage that is clearly inconsistent with life.

In the case of electrocution, cardiopulmonary resuscitation (CPR) for an hour or longer can allow stunned nerves to recover, allowing an apparently dead person to survive. Likewise, people found unconscious under icy water may survive if their faces are left continuously cold until they arrive at an emergency room.

Following death, in animals, small movements of the limbs like twitching legs or wings can sometimes be observed. This is known as postmortem spasm.

Pallor mortis is the condition in which postmortem paleness accompanies death due to a lack of capillary circulation throughout the body.

Algor mortis describes the predictable decline in body temperature until ambient temperature is reached.

Within a few hours of death, chemical changes in the muscles causes the limbs of the corpse to become stiff and difficult to move or manipulate. This is known as rigor mortis and usually occurs at about twelve hours eventually subsiding to relaxation at about thirty-six hours.

Death rattle is a gurgling or rattle-like noise produced shortly before or after death by the accumulation of excessive respiratory secretions in the throat. Those who are dying may lose their ability to swallow, resulting in such an accumulation.

Death erection or terminal erection is a postmortem erection, technically a priapism, is generally observed in corpses of human males who have been executed, particularly by hanging. This phenomenon has been attributed to pressure on the cerebellum created by the noose. Spinal cord injuries are known to be associated with priapism. In fact, injuries to the cerebellum or spinal cord are often associated with priapism in living patients. In women, the labia will become engorged and there may be discharge of blood from the vagina.

The major causes of death world-wide are on account of cardiovascular diseases involving heart or blood vessels (29.34%), infectious and parasitic diseases (19.12%), ischemic heart diseases which result in reduced blood supply to the heart muscles (12.64%), cancers (12.49%), strokes (9.66%), respiratory infections (6.95%) and AIDS/HIV (4.87%).

What is extension of life?

This refers to slowing down or reversing the processes of aging. Theoretically, extension of maximum life span can be achieved by reducing the rate of aging damage, by periodic replacement of damaged tissues, or by molecular repair or rejuvenation of deteriorated cells and tissues. Many biomedical gerontologists and life extensionists believe that future breakthroughs in tissue rejuvenation with stem cells, organ replacements and molecular repair will eliminate all aging and diseases as well as allow for complete rejuvenation to a youthful condition. Some life extensionists arrange to be cryonically preserved upon 'legal death' so that they can await the time when future medicines can eliminate disease, rejuvenate them to a lasting youthful condition and repair damage caused by the cyronics process.

How do we dispose of the dead body?

Decomposition sets in at the moment of death. Two factors are responsible for this process. The first one is autolysis which is essentially breaking down of tissues by the body's own internal chemicals and enzymes. The second one is putrefaction caused by breakdown of tissues by bacteria.

In any case, these processes have the effect of releasing gases that are the chief source of the characteristic odour of dead bodies. These gases also swell the body.

Burial or inhumation is the act of placing a person or object into the ground. Human burial practices are the manifestation of the human desire to demonstrate 'respect for the dead.' If the body is not buried, scavengers may eat the corpse. It is also an attempt to bring closure to the deceased's family and friends by interring a body away from plain view, thereby lessening the pain of losing a loved one. As many cultures believe in afterlife, burial is often believed to be a necessary step for an individual to reach the afterlife. The act of burying corpses is thought to have begun around 200,000 years ago during the Paleolithic period by homo-sapiens, before spreading out from Africa.

In a 'Natural Burial', the body is returned to nature in a biodegradable coffin or shroud. Native vegetation (often a memorial tree) is planted over or near the grave in lieu of a conventional cemetery monument. This practice dates back to the late 19th century, when Sir Francis Hayden proposed 'earth to earth burial.' Muslims practice natural burials with the deceased's body covered in shroud and with his/her face facing Mecca. Inclusion of personal effects or grave goods may be motivated by the belief that in the afterlife a person will wish to keep with him what was important to him on earth.

Christian burials are normally supine in which the deceased lies on his back with either his arms and legs straight or with the arms folded upon the chest, and with the eyes and mouth closed. The head is at the western end of the grave. There are cases of other body positions like prone, flexed with the legs folded up to the chest, upright and mass burials in which the bodies may be positioned arbitrarily. In inverted burials, the head is vertically below the feet. This is highly unusual and generally symbolic. Occasionally, suicide cases were buried upside down, as a postmortem punishment and to inhibit such kind of activity for the undead.

African-American slaves were buried with the head facing east and feet west. This positioning represented the ability to rise without having to turn around at the call of Gabriel's trumpet which would be blown in the eastern sunrise. This positioning also was the direction of home, Africa.

All such burials were typically at night when the workday was over.

The Bahai's faith prescribes both the location of burial practices and procedures. It is forbidden to carry the body for more than one hour's journey from the place of death. Before interment, the body should be wrapped in a shroud of silk or cotton, and a ring should be placed on its finger bearing the following inscription:

> 'I came forth from God, and return unto Him, holding fast to his Name, the Merciful, the Compassionate.'

The coffin should be of crystal, stone or hard fine wood. However, these procedures are applicable to those dead over fifteen years of age.

Apart from burials, there are other interesting methods of disposal round the world.

In the French penal settlement of Devil's Island, the dead prisoners were thrown to the sharks at 4 pm.

Some indigenous Australian and Native American cultures expose the body on a platform or in trees for some time to decompose. Later, they would collect the bones for burial.

In Solomon Islands, the bodies are left in canoes to decompose or placed on a reef to be consumed by sharks. They regard death with suspicion and never seen as accidental, but the result of angry and evil spirits. The skulls were collected and stored in wooden effigies, model canoes or in mortuary huts and on stone altars.

The Masai of Kenya relied on hyenas to dispose off the dead.The Djurs of Sudan placed the body of the deceased on a termite nest so that the flesh could be stripped from the bones.

Zoroastrians of India and Iran feed the bodies of their dead to vultures. Because of paucity of vultures to consume all the bodies, the Parsi Council in Mumbai has installed giant solar reflectors to hasten the process of decomposition of corpses.

Currently, in Mumbai, on an average, three Parsees die every day. A handful of vultures available at the Tower of Silence are already overfed.

Experts have opined that about 100–120 birds would be needed to deal with the daily intake of bodies. The body of a deceased person, believed to be contaminated by Nasu (decomposition) must only be prepared and transported by special people called Nassesalars.

The corpse must be disposed off as quickly and efficiently as possible, and preferably without coming in contact with fire, water or the earth.

Dokhma is a circular stone tower which is open to the sky to allow sunlight and birds of prey to enter.

The design allows for the drainage of body fluids to drain through the central well, which only the corpse-bearers are permitted to enter.

Thupten Tashi, a former Buddhist monk, had once observed:

> 'After death, the person has left the body and their mind or concious-ness has traveled. This body cannot be serviceable without concious-ness. So once the mind has left, the body becomes rotten like a dead tree. Dead trees are only useful for burning.'

The Tibetans believe that death is not something to fear. They believe in life as a cycle of birth, death and rebirth. They have the belief that after death, the consciousness remains in an intermediate stage known as Bardo, a state between death and rebirth, for up to 49 days.

The Tibetans either cremate their dead or expose the body to carrion-feeders like vultures. The corpse cutters throw pieces of flesh to these birds. The human bones, like the thigh bone or femur and skull, are often used for creating the necessary sounds during important rituals. This perhaps helps in dispelling fear about death. Hindus cremate their dead, believing that the burning of a dead body signifies the release of the spirit and the flames represent Brahma, the creator.

In Hindu religion, fire is considered as a sacred gateway to the spiritual world. Cremation of a body has to occur preferably within six hours of the person's death in the simplest ceremonial way. The corpse is usually bathed and dressed in white, the traditional Indian cloth. If the wife dies before her husband, she is dressed in red bridal clothes. If the woman is a widow, she will be dressed in white or pale colours. The pyre is lit either by the eldest son (in case of father) or the younger son (in the case of mother).

After the corpse is almost completely burnt, the chief mourner performs the rite called *Kapalakriya*, the 'rite of the skull'. Cracking the skull with a long bamboo stick is said to release the soul from entrapment in the body.

In the case of disposal of a body in an electric crematorium, the casket is put on the top level of the cremator's chamber and then burnt. When the body is burnt, bones and calcium deposits drop through to the second level of the chamber. It takes one to one and a half hours for the body to be completely burnt at a heat source of 900 degrees centigrade.

About 80 kg will burn each hour. Only one body can be cremated at a time. When the remains are cooled, they are scanned for metallic prostheses and coffin components. Bones and calcium deposits are milled down to finer particles in a grinder. The ashes weigh around 2 kg and are available to relatives 24 hours after cremation.

Death rituals do not end here. After the funeral, everyone undergoes a 'purifying' bath. The immediate family members remain in a state of intense pollution for a set number of days. To ensure the safe passage of the spirit of the dead person to the Otherworld, an eleven-day ritual called *Shraddh* is performed. It consists of daily offerings of rice balls called *Pindas*, which pacify the soul so that it will not linger longer in this world as a ghost but will pass through to the world of his ancestors, or the 'far shore.' On the 12th day, the departed soul is said to reach its destination and be joined with its ancestors, a fact expressed by symbolically joining a small *Pinda* to a much larger one.

Shraddh is again practised one year after the death of a person. It can either be an annual event or a large one-off event. This is the Hindu practice of giving food to the poor in memory of the deceased. A priest will say prayers for the deceased and during this time, usually lasting one month, the family will abstain from socializing, making new purchases and shifting residence. Sons are responsible for performing *Shraddh*.

A word about decomposition of a body.

Flies are first on the scene. They prefer a moist corpse for the maggots to feed on, as such a corpse is easier for them to chew. Beetles are generally found on the corpse when it is more decomposed. While Mites feed on a corpse, Moths are amongst the last animals contributing to the decomposition of a corpse.

A basic guide for the effect of environment on decomposition is given as Casper's Law (or Ratio): where there is free access of air a body decomposes twice as fast than if immersed in water and eight times faster than if buried in earth.

On a surface in tropical areas, invertebrates alone can reduce a fully fleshed corpse to clean bones in about two weeks. The skeleton itself is not permanent as acids in the soil can reduce it to unrecognizable components. In extremely dry or cold conditions, the normal process of decomposition is slowed down enabling the body to be preserved as a mummy. Frozen mummies commonly restart the decomposition process when thawed, while heat-desiccated mummies remain so unless exposed to moisture.

Bodies of newborns which have never ingested food are an important exception to the normal process of decomposition as they lack the internal microbial flora that cause much of the decomposition. They quite commonly mummify if kept in even moderately dry conditions.

Embalming is the practice of delaying decomposition of human and animal remains. It slows decomposition somewhat, but does not forestall it indefinitely. The chemicals used in embalming repel most insects and slows down bacterial putrefaction by 'fixing' cellular proteins, which prevents them from acting as a nutrient for bacteria, apart from killing the bacteria itself.

In sufficiently dry environments, an embalmed body may end up mummified and it is not uncommon for bodies in dry vaults to remain preserved to a viewable extent after decades. The body of Lenin was kept submerged in a special tank of fluids for decades, almost perfectly preserved. Bodies submerged in peat bog (accumulation of partially decayed vegetation matter) may become naturally 'embalmed', averting decomposition and resulting in a preserved specimen known as bog body. The preserved body of Evita Peron is one such example of a bog body.

3

REINCARNATION

Reincarnation literally means 'to be made flesh again.' This belief is an ancient one. This doctrine is the central tenet within the majority of Indian religious traditions such as Hinduism, Jainism and Sikhism. This doctrine is not the monopoly of India alone. That some traces of such a thought can be seen in the records of other nations like the Greeks and that even the Bible is not inconsistent with such a belief.

But it is in India that the thought was developed in a rational and systematic way. It is to this extent that the doctrine is unique in Indian thought. As stated, this idea was also entertained by some ancient Greek philosophers.

Many modern Pagans (country dwellers, rustics) also believe in reincarnation as do some New Age movements. It is also believed by students of esoteric philosophy (one which is specialized or advanced in nature, available only to a narrow circle of 'enlightened, initiated or highly educated people') such as Kabbalah, Sufism, Gnostic and Esoteric Christianity. Kabbalah is the name applied to the whole range of Jewish mystical activity. Holy Kabbalah is the 'hidden' or 'secret' teachings of Judaism.

The idea of reincarnation, however, has never been fully accepted by Christianity because it undermines its basic tenets. Firstly, it compromises God's sovereignty over creation, transforming him into a helpless spectator of the human tragedy. There is, thus, no need for the impersonal law of Karma and for reincarnation to play this role.

Secondly, belief in reincarnation may affect one's understanding of morality and motivation for moral living. An extreme application of reincarnationist convictions could lead to adopting a detached stand to crime, theft and other social plagues. They could be considered nothing else but normal debts to be paid by their victims, which originated in previous lives.

Lastly, reincarnation represents a threat to the very essence of Christianity: the need for Christ's redemptive sacrifice for our sins. If we are to pay for the consequences of our sins ourselves in further lives and attain salvation through our own efforts, the sacrifice of Christ becomes useless and absurd. In this case, Christianity would be a mere form of Hindu Bhakti-Yoga.

According to Vedic anthropology, the components of human nature are the physical body, *ashu* and *manas*. *Ashu* represents the vital principle (different from personal attributes), and *manas* the sum of psycho-mental faculties (mind, feeling and will).

The belief in the preservation of the three components after death is proved by the fact that the family addressed the departed relative in the burial ritual as a unitary person: 'May nothing of your *manas*, nothing of the *ashu*, nothing of the limbs, nothing of your vital fluid, nothing of your body here by any means be lost' (*Atharva Veda* 18,2,24).

The premise of reaping the reward of one's life in a new earthly existence (instead of a heavenly afterlife) appeared in the *Brahmana* writings (9th century BC). They spoke of a limited heavenly immortality, depending on the deeds and the quality of the sacrifices performed during one's life. After reaping the reward for them, humans have to face a second death in the heavenly realm (*punarmrityu*) and, thereafter, return to an earthly existence. The proper antidote to this fate came to be considered esoteric knowledge, attainable only during one's earthly existence.

In India, the concept of reincarnation was first recorded in the Upanishads (c 800 BCE) which are philosophical and religious texts composed in Sanskrit. The Upanishads were the first writings to move the place of one's 'second death' from the heavenly realm to this earthly world and to consider its proper solution to be the knowledge of the *atman–Brahman* identity.

The Upanishads gave a new meaning of afterlife from the Vedic perspective. It abandoned the goal of having communion with the gods, attained as a result of bringing good sacrifices, and came to consider man's final destiny to be the impersonal fusion *atman–Brahman*, attained exclusively by esoteric knowledge. In this new context, Karma and reincarnation are key elements that will define all particular developments in Hinduism.

According to Hinduism, the soul (*atman*) is immortal, while the body is subject to birth and death. The entity that reincarnates is the impersonal self. The *Gita* states as under:

> 'Worn out garments are shed by the body; worn-out bodies are shed by the dweller within the body. New bodies are donned by the dweller, like garments.'

There is some permanent element in an embodied person joined to an impermanent element called the body. The permanent element is the soul. Before the soul assumed a particular body, that soul had been in some earlier body, rather in a series of earlier bodies.

Closely associated with this is the doctrine that a man assumes a particular body with particular traits and aptitudes in consequence of his actions and in a prior embodied state.

Karma is the term usually applied to this experience in a specific state and its causal relation with a prior act on the part of the man.

The doctrine of Karma and of the Transmigration of the Soul should be traced to the fundamental doctrine of the independence of Man and of the world, God being only a factor in the scheme of the world and not an Overlord of the world, if there is a God.

In other systems of religion and philosophy, Man is absolutely a subordinate factor in the Universe and it is the will of the Almighty that prevails. The *Puranas* developed this topic in greater detail in as much as even specific destinies were worked out according to each kind of 'sin' that one commits:

> 'The murderer of a Brahmin becomes consumptive, the killer of a cow becomes hump-backed and imbecile, the murderer of a virgin becomes leprous—all three born as outcastes. The slayer of a woman and the destroyer of embryos becomes a savage full of diseases; who commits illicit intercourse, a eunuch; who goes with his teacher's wife, disease-skinned. The eater of flesh becomes very red; the drinker of intoxicants, one with discolored teeth... Who steals food becomes a rat; who steals grain becomes a locust... perfumes, a musk rat; honey, a gadfly; flesh, a vulture; and salt, an ant... Who commits unnatural vice becomes a village pig; who consorts with a Sudra woman becomes a bull; who is passionate becomes a lustful horse... These and other signs and births are seen to be the karma of the embodied, made by

> themselves in this world. Thus, the makers of bad Karma, having experienced the tortures of hell, are reborn with the residues of their sins, in these stated forms (*Garuda Purana* 5).

The idea that the soul (of any living being including animals, humans and plants) reincarnates is intricately linked to Karma. The cycle of birth and death, governed by Karma, is referred to as *Samsara*. According to Adi Shankaracharya, the world as we ordinarily understand it is like a dream: fleeting and illusory. To be trapped in *Samsara* is a result of ignorance and the true nature of our existence.

When the cycle of rebirth finally comes to an end, a person is said to have attained *Moksha* or salvation. When all desires have vanished, the person will not be reborn anymore.

The Sikhs believe that the soul has to transmigrate from one body to another as part of an evolution process of the soul. This evolution of the soul will eventually result in a union with God upon the proper purification of the spirit. If one does not perform righteous deeds, one's soul will continue to cycle in reincarnation forever. A being who has performed good deeds and actions in his or her life is transmigrated to a better and higher life form in the next life until the soul of the being becomes Godlike. From a human life form, if one performs the proper functions of a *Gurmukh* (meaning 'to follow the ways of the Guru' and not to follow your animal instincts and baser designs of your mind), the person can achieve salvation with God. One must cleanse the soul by reciting *Naam*, by remembrance of *Waheguru* (meaning 'Wonderful Lord' in Punjabi and also known as *Onkar*, *Satguru*, *Satnaam*, *Rabh* and *Preetam*) and by following the path of Gurmat (tenets of the Guru).

Jains follow the teachings of the twenty four *Jinas* (conquerors) who are also known as Tirthankars. The 24th of them, Mahavira, lived in c 600 BC. One of the main characteristics of Jain beliefs is the emphasis on Karma. Essentially, it means that all '*jivas*' reap what they sow.

Jains do not accept the authority of the Vedas and do not regard God as a creator. The Jain idea of Godhood is the perfect soul (*Siddha*) and the liberated soul (*Mukta*). The Jains worship these liberated souls (*Tirthankaras*) who have destroyed all Karma and attained salvation, as their God. Jainism believes that each soul has a separate individuality, uncreated and eternal in existence. It takes fresh bodies after death so long as the Karmas generated in previous lives have not been fully worked out. Eventually it unfolds its absolute purity by breaking the bond of Karma and attains perfection, Nirvana or *Mukti*.

When all the good and evil deeds are eliminated, one attains emancipation or *Moksha* which is the total elimination of Karma from the *Jiva*.

The *Jiva* gets freedom as soon as it attains this stage. The liberated soul goes to the abode *Siddhakshetra*, which is at the top of the world. The soul becomes pure by the removal of matter. In this condition, there is no pain, misery, disease, old age or death. It is a condition of immortality, infinite knowledge and eternal uninterrupted bliss.

Quite clearly, Jainism believes in reincarnation.

Buddhism explains rebirth as a cycle of consciousness. This is consistent with the other core Buddhist beliefs like *Annica* (impermanence), *Dukkha* (unsatisfactoriness) and *Anatta* (non-self). Rebirth in Buddhism is the doctrine that the consciousness of a person; upon the death or dissolution of the aggregates (*Skandhas*) which make up that person, becomes one of the contributing causes for the arising of a new group of *Skandhas* which may again be conventionally considered a person or individual.

Buddhists see our present life as a causal continuum. It is a bit like the flow of a river. This flow that we are is made of five strands: physical matter, sensation, determinate perception and additional factors like volition (intention) and consciousness. These are the five aggregates or *Skandhas*. Upon this fivefold flow, we superimpose for everyday practical purposes a singular identity, called by a name of an individual.

Death is merely a particular sort of break caused in the physical flow. A crucial element which distinguishes it from those held by Hindus, is that the element of the individual that precedes birth and survives death is not a fixed and permanent entity. The habitual tendencies—the patterns, developed and modified by action in the course of this life are passed onto the next, and nothing else and not surely the ledger of good and bad Karmas accumulated by the individual concerned in his previous birth(s). There is no fixed core that can be called a 'soul' or an 'I'. The 'I' that we experience is actually our awareness of this complex set of habitual tendencies which have formed themselves into a sort of knot.

Until Enlightenment is reached, the knot always exists, but its constituent contents can change. It is this 'knot' that passes from one life to the next.

While all Buddhist traditions seem to accept some notion of rebirth, there is no unified view about precisely how events unfold after the moment of death.

Theravada Buddhism generally asserts that rebirth is immediate. The Tibetan schools, on the other hand, hold to the notion of a *bardo* (intermediate state) which can last up to 49 days.

Some earlier Buddhist texts like *Sarvastivada* believed that between death and rebirth there is a sort of limbo in which beings do not yet reap the consequences of their previous actions but in which they may still influence their rebirth.

The death process and this intermediate state were believed to offer a uniquely favourable opportunity for spiritual awakening. An important scripture of Taoism, the Ch Chuang Tzu (4th century BC) states:

> 'Birth is not a beginning; death is not an end. There is existence without limitation; there is continuity without a starting point. Existence without limitation is space. Continuity without a starting point is time. There is birth, there is death, there is issuing forth, there

is entering in. That through which one passes in and out without seeing its form, that is the Portal of the Divine.'

Quite clearly, Taoism did believe in reincarnation.

The Tibetan Book of the Dead describes in detail the experiences one has in the intermediary state between two reincarnations, suggesting that the deceased keeps some personal attributes.

Although it is not clear what actually survives after death in this case, it mentions a mental body that cannot be injured by the visions experienced by the deceased:

> 'When it happens that such a vision arises, do not be afraid! Do not feel terror! You have a mental body made of instincts; even if it is killed or dismembered, it cannot die! Since in fact you are a natural form of voidness, anger at being injured is unnecessary! The Yama Lords of Death are but arisen from the natural energy of your own

> awareness and really lack all substantiality. Voidness cannot injure voidness!' (Tibetan Book of the Dead, 12)

Whatever the condition of the deceased after life may be, any hypothetical personal nucleus vanishes just before birth, so there can be no psycho-mental element transmitted from one life to another. The newborn person doesn't remember anything from previous lives or trips into the realm of the intermediary state (*bardo*).

Pythagoras claimed that he could remember his past lives. An association between Pythogorean philosophy and reincarnation was routinely accepted throughout antiquity. Socrates said at the end of his life:

> 'I am confident that there truly is such a thing as living again, and that the living spring from the death.'

Greek Platonism asserted the pre-existence of the soul in a celestial world and its fall into a human body due to sin. In order to be liberated from its bondage and return to a state of pure being, the soul needs to be purified through reincarnation. In stating such beliefs, Plato was strongly influenced by the earlier philosophical schools of Orphism and Pythagoreanism.

The first important Greek philosophical system that adopted a view on reincarnation similar to that of Hinduism was Neo-Platonism, in the 3rd century AD, under certain Eastern influences.

In the Hermetica, a Graeco-Egyptian series of writings on cosmology and spirituality attributed to Hermes Trismegistus/Thoth, the doctrine of reincarnation is central.

In the case of ancient Egypt, The Egyptian Book of the Dead describes the travel of the soul into the next world without making any allusions to its return to earth.

The ancient Egyptians embalmed the dead in order that the body might be preserved and accompany the soul into that world. This suggests their belief in resurrection rather than in reincarnation.

Reincarnation has been a part of Judaism since at least the time of Flavius Josephus' War of the Jews (CE 66–73). The idea of reincarnation called 'Gilgul' became popular in folk belief, and is found in much Yiddish literature among the Ashkenazi Jews. A quote from the Sephar ha Zohar is as under:

> 'The souls must re-enter the Absolute, from where they have emerged. But to accomplish this they must develop the perfection; the germ of which is planted in them. And if they have not developed these traits in this one life, then they must commence another, a third, and so forth. They must go on like this until they acquire the conditions that allow them to associate again with God—The Zohar.

Mainstream Islam rejects the idea of reincarnation but a number of Sufi groups do believe in it.

As would be seen, Judaism, Christianity and Islam believe life and death to be linear: a being is born (usually understood as a new creation), live and then die, at which point their soul or other part that survives death, passes to a domain that is inaccessible to living beings and remains there indefinitely, or until the end of the world.

The dominant view of these traditions is that the soul of the individual comes into being at conception. It lives but one short life on this earth, and then, after divine judgement, is awarded eternal happiness in heaven, or eternal suffering in hell.

Note that reincarnation, in the limited form of Gilgul Neshamot plays a role in some form of Judaism as does Sufism in the context of Islam and Gnostics in relation to Christianity.

Druze, a branch of Ismailism, do not consider themselves either Arabs nor Muslims. They do not intermarry with Muslims and Jews. This small religious community has members in Syria, Lebanon and Israel. However, they have a restricted belief in reincarnation (*tanasukh*).

Reincarnation is, however, an intrinsic part of many Native North

American and Inuit traditions. It also appears in Norse mythology, in the Poetic Edda and was commonplace among the Vikings.

Can we deny or accept the concept of reincarnation?

Reincarnation has been a subject that has fascinated the human race for almost as long as there has been a human race! There have been many references to reincarnation in the writings of most civilizations throughout the ages. Eastern religions accept it more readily than western. There are people who believe and claim to have evidence that the Bible had many references to reincarnation before it was 'rewritten'.

Reincarnation is a highly debated issue and brings out strong opinions especially amongst the scientific community. Some believe this fascination is only because of our fear of death—our fear of ceasing to exist without the possibility of being created again. Perhaps reincarnation offers a slim ray of hope of being born again albeit in a different form.

For most people, reincarnation is a matter of faith. Millions of Hindus and people from some other religious denominations believe in it. Some polls show that over 20 per cent of Americans, who self-identify as Christians do too, despite Christianity's repudiation of the idea. In fact, reincarnation is an idea that Jesus himself once declined an opportunity to refute.

According to Vedic literature, the psychophysical entity with which we now identify ourselves is not our true self. The true self is neither the body nor the mind, nor a combination of both. The Vedic sages tell us that the body and mind are but gross and subtle coverings of the self. Underlying these temporary coverings, the real self is a spark of spiritual consciousness, eternal and unchanging but temporarily misidentifying itself with matter in the form of the body and mind. And this real self survives the death of the body and lives on. Where does it go?

The Vedic answer is that at the end of one life time, we embark upon another unless we have achieved *Moksha*. How does reincarnation work?

According to the *Gita*, whatever we think at the time of death determines what sort of body we'll take next. The *Gita* further explains that the mind, at death, carries with it subtle conceptions, just as the air carries aromas. And these subtle thoughts are what shape the next body. If reincarnation is real, why can we not recall our past lives?

Srimad-Bhagavatam, a Vedic scripture, has an answer. It says that by the trauma of birth, a child forgets his previous life. If reincarnation is a fact, why is the population increasing? According to Vedic literature, there are as many as 8,400,000 species of life and living beings pass through all of them. The truth of this Vedic teaching is beyond the ability of science to either confirm or deny. Reincarnation is actually being studied scientifically today.

Categories

The research falls in the following three categories:

Children's claim of past life memories

Dr Ian Stevenson has spent nearly 40 years of his life globe-trotting, following up on thousands of cases of very young children who reported intricate details of their past lives. Stevenson reported that in 51 per cent of the cases, the 'previous person' had met with a violent death.

Skeptics say that majority of such cases occur in countries whose people believe in reincarnation. Stevenson himself admits that his studies are merely 'suggestive' of reincarnation but declines to state positively whether reincarnation is real.

Birthmark Matches

Studies have suggested a connection between birthmarks and injuries from past lives.

Skeptics again aver that location and pattern of birthmarks is simply a matter of chance.

Past Life Regression by Adults

Some believe that memories which surface during hypnotherapy sessions offer evidence of a person's past life.

Skeptics offer a different view. They say that a subject may describe a life in ancient times with great emotion, but since the statement cannot be verified as accurate for a particular individual who actually lived, the evidential value of such a case is very limited at best.

What then is the truth?

It is indeed an extremely difficult and complicated field in the near absence of any concrete evidence. Though research is being carried out, there are severe inherent limitations to its extent and veracity. This is so because no one has yet 'returned' from the Land of the Dead for any sort of debriefing. It is only a one-way ticket.

In reel life, Boris Karloff did try to tell his 'experience of life after death' in an old film called The Walking Dead but died before he could enlighten anyone about it. It is unlikely that, apart from sketchy empirical evidence which is at best suggestive, any hard evidence would be available, as for now or in the foreseeable future.

How does this square up with the religious belief(s) especially in Eastern religions?

The answer lies in the query itself. Reincarnation is, as of now, strictly a matter of belief. All of us would perhaps know the answer but only when one passes on from our earthly existence.

But again, to whom do we confirm or deny the ultimate truth except perhaps to the peer group of the deceased themselves?